www.providencebooks.net

Publisher Contact

Email:contact@providencebooks.net

Social media: facebook.com/providencebooks

Acknowledgements

The team at Providence Books would like to thank our friends, family, suppliers and customers for making our vision of creating the highest-quality books a reality. Thanks for purchasing and enjoy the quotes!

This page is intentionally left blank

This page is intentionally left blank

A friend of my mom's was a casting director so, really as kind of a lark, I had a couple of acting jobs that had just enough exposure to give me the option to continue if I wanted to. I followed through with it.

Ben Affleck

After 2000 or so, I started to realize I wanted to be doing something else. I didn't want to be in front of a camera. I was frustrated. I didn't think I would stop acting, but I didn't want to be seen.

Ben Affleck

All I do, really, is go to work and try to be professional, be on time and be prepared.

Ben Affleck

Anxiety is a kind of fuel that activates the fight-or-flight part of the brain in me. It makes sure that a velociraptor isn't around the corner and that you do as much as you possibly can to survive. Because Hollywood has a lot in common with 'Jurassic Park' and its primeval-dinosaur universe.

Ben Affleck

As an actor, you can steer a scene in another direction by playing it a little differently. And honestly? I like being an actor, and I want to keep having a career.

Ben Affleck

But when I felt like I had something to prove? Then I got up early every morning and worked all day long. I didn't know if I had any more talent than anyone else directing, but I knew I could work hard at it, and so I did.

Ben Affleck

Every single director-actor I talked to, from Warren Beatty to Clint Eastwood to George Clooney, said the biggest mistake they made is not shooting enough footage of themselves.

Ben Affleck

Everyone's entitled to express their political beliefs. I don't presume to tell anybody who to vote for. I am comfortable telling people what my opinions are.

Ben Affleck

God help me if I ever do another movie with an explosion in it. If you see me in a movie where stuff is exploding you'll know I've lost all my money.

Ben Affleck

I didn't do anything for two years but work on 'Gone Baby Gone,' and it was miserable and hard, but at the end? It is a good movie. I liked it very much. If it had been dismissed and deemed worthless, it would been definitely devastating. But that didn't happen.

Ben Affleck

I feel like fame is wasted on me.

Ben Affleck

I find forgiveness to be really healthy.

Ben Affleck

I got into acting as a young child on account of a sort of arbitrary thing. A friend of my mom's was a casting director, so really, as kind of a lark, I had a couple of acting jobs that had just enough exposure to give me the option to continue if I wanted to. I followed through with it.

Ben Affleck

I grew up in a home environment where I wasn't getting esteem for anything I did.

Ben Affleck

I grew up in a house with a mother who was a teacher and a Freedom Rider - very left-wing Democrats living in a heterogeneous working-class neighborhood. I picked up a lot of those values there, and I brought them with me when I showed up in Hollywood.

Ben Affleck

I hate the whole reluctant sex-symbol thing. It's such bull. You see these dudes greased up, in their underwear, talking about how they don't want to be a sex symbol.

Ben Affleck

I have a good relationship with the world. But I don't know what the trick is to maintaining it.

Ben Affleck

I have a lot of influences. I like to sit down with the cinematographer a month before, and we'll watch pieces of 20 or 30 movies. You're basically the sum of all the experiences you've ever had, and they're sort of shaken up in you and reproduced in the things you create, and that includes seeing movies.

Ben Affleck

I just feel like sometimes I'm a force to be dealt with. My talents are sometimes overused and also sometimes underused. It's not easy being me.

Ben Affleck

I kinda see my current position like this: Here's your five minutes in the toy store, so you gotta do all the good movies you can before 'Chuck Woolery' rings the bell.

Ben Affleck

I knew I had to get out of Boston and stop making movies there, at least for one movie, otherwise no one would ever consider me for a movie that took place south of Providence.

Ben Affleck

I like acting for myself as a director. I act and I know that I'll have a chance to have some say in what gets used and that I'll be able to give myself enough takes and be on the same page as myself about how the scene should play.

Ben Affleck

I like roundtables because you can talk more directly to people. And you also can get kind of a vibe on what a journalist's take is on something, and have a conversation with them more.

Ben Affleck

I like to think that if I were gay I would be out. Rupert Everett-style.

Ben Affleck

I lived with this tremendous fear of failure because my father was a playwright and a director, and I think he did a couple of things as a child as an actor as well, and he... he failed, basically.

Ben Affleck

I really think that everybody would like to be an actor. Why wouldn't they? It's great work if you can get it. The one thing that prevents most people from saying, 'I'm just gonna go to Hollywood!' is that it seems unrealistic.

Ben Affleck

I remember back when I was a kid there was a comic strip called Plastic Man. His body was elastic and he could make his extremities as long as he wanted. As a youngster I didn't fully appreciate. But I'm now thinking Plastic Man was probably pretty popular with the ladies.

Ben Affleck

I started as a child, in this PBS series 'Voyage of the Mimi,' which led to driving down to New York for 'Afterschool Special' auditions, which led to moving to Los Angeles. I wanted to be an actor. But in L.A., I got into film technology, and I was building cheap editing systems and would edit my friend's acting reels.

Ben Affleck

I went to the University of Vermont because I had a kind of unrequited love for this high school girlfriend. She wasn't even at the University but at another school nearby. But I thought if went to a school near her, just maybe... I was really remedial about girls in so many ways.

Ben Affleck

I'm a writer. An amateur photographer. An actor.

Ben Affleck

I'm always described as 'cocksure' or 'with a swagger,' and that bears no resemblance to who I feel like inside. I feel plagued by insecurity.

Ben Affleck

I'm human, just like anybody else.

Ben Affleck

I'm much more interested in what an actor has to say about something substantial and important than who they're dating or what clothes they're wearing or some other asinine, insignificant aspect of their life.

Ben Affleck

I'm not the most loathsome man in the world. I've dropped to number nine.

Ben Affleck

I'm not the type of guy who enjoys one-night stands. It leaves me feeling very empty and cynical. It's not even fun sexually. I need to feel something for the woman and entertain the vain hope that it may lead to a relationship.

Ben Affleck

I'm sure I can make a movie that doesn't feel like a seventies movie! But the truth is, that's my favorite era in American filmmaking. To me, those were the great years.

Ben Affleck

I'm very insecure. I'm human, just like anybody else.

Ben Affleck

I've consciously taken on material that's a bit too much for me but not an overreach. The first movie, just about performances. 'The Town,' I learned how to work broader material, develop tension, direct bigger scenes, action sequences. 'Argo,' I experimented with film stock, widened the scope of my geography.

Ben Affleck

I've finally learnt how to say, 'No comment'. To appear in the tabloids is a real learning curve and a steep one at that. You had better learn quick or you get burnt.

Ben Affleck

I've learned to think, I may succeed or fail, but I'm going to do so on the merit of my own instincts.

Ben Affleck

I've never held myself up particularly high when I had movies that worked, and I never held myself all that low when I had failures.

Ben Affleck

If I ever woke up with a dead hooker in my hotel room, Matt would be the first person I'd call.

Ben Affleck

In our culture, we get very much into shorthanding people. And I got shorthanded as That Guy: Jennifer Lopez, movies bombed, therefore he must be a sort of thoughtless dilettante, solipsistic consumer blahblahblah. It's hard to shake those sort of narratives.

Ben Affleck

It was a dreamlike time for me from December 1997 to March of '98. Before that, I was basically unknown. Then, bang! The starting gun fired, and everybody just started running. It was learn-on-the-job. And there were more opportunities for work than I had time to do them.

Ben Affleck

It's wrong and disgusting to follow children around and take their picture and sell it for money.

Ben Affleck

Making movies has become such a golden ring, and it's all such a big business, that the rewards system has gotten totally out of whack. Suddenly, you're treated in a manner befitting someone who is actually an important person.

Ben Affleck

Marriage hasn't been my thing. But gay people, knock yourselves out!

Ben Affleck

My father has positional vertigo, and if he flies he gets really dizzy, so he has to drive out to California, which he does a couple times a year. We talk, but we e-mail mostly.

Ben Affleck

My kids aren't celebrities. They never made that bargain. We were offered a lot of money to sell pictures of our kids when they were born. You'll notice there aren't any. I make no judgment about people who decide differently; a lot of them give the money to charity. For me, it was a matter of principle.

Ben Affleck

My mother gets all mad at me if I stay in a hotel. I'm 31-years-old, and I don't want to sleep on a sleeping bag down in the basement. It's humiliating.

Ben Affleck

My mother taught public school, went to Harvard and then got her master's there and taught fifth and sixth grade in a public school. My dad had a more working-class lifestyle. He didn't go to college. He was an auto mechanic and a bartender and a janitor at Harvard.

Ben Affleck

My movies are unadorned, they're not particularly fancy, I think they're kind of workmanlike in some ways, focusing on the writing and the acting.

Ben Affleck

Narcissism is the part of my personality that I am the least proud of, and I certainly don't like to see it highlighted in everybody else I meet.

Ben Affleck

Nobody I represent is pretending to be the pope or a role model for young people. People have to live their lives. They have the right to smoke if they want.

Ben Affleck

Not that it entirely matters: There is a perception that all actors make their movies. A lot of people assume you're responsible. George Clooney told me actors get all of the blame and all the credit.

Ben Affleck

One guy told me I was a great actor, I just would never be on the cover of a magazine.

Ben Affleck

People decided that I was the frat guy, even though I've never been inside a fraternity, or the guy who beat them up at school, even though that wasn't me at all.

Ben Affleck

People of similar political persuasions tend to flock together.

Ben Affleck

Rumors about me? Calista Flockhart, Pam Anderson, and Matt Damon. That's who I'm dating.

Ben Affleck

Sometimes I get insecure about being a real director because I look at the great directors, and they have such command. But maybe that keeps me critical of myself. Maybe it keeps me moving forward.

Ben Affleck

Sure, I suffered a lot. But it's not like the end of the world and it's not who I am. I lead quite a pleasant life and I'm able to divorce a perceived reality from my actual experience of life.

Ben Affleck

The first 'Star Wars' movie had come out in 1977 and had become this huge phenomenon with all the toys and everything - it just kind of swept America. But internationally, it was also a big deal.

Ben Affleck

The first day of 'The Town' was one of the most satisfying days of my career.

Ben Affleck

The first thing that I really understood politically and was old enough to get was the failed assassination attempt on Reagan.

Ben Affleck

The one benefit of having done all kinds of movies as an actor is, you learn the pros and cons of being tempted to do a really big movie because it costs a lot of money.

Ben Affleck

The trap for an actor is that you become too successful at what you're trying to do, and you can find yourself stuck there.

Ben Affleck

There is nothing worse that a thirteen-year-old boy. You're embarrassed by your parents, and you're trying to find your independance because, deep inside, you are so dependent on your mom.

Ben Affleck

There's a lot of crazy, weird people out there. It's an ugly world.

Ben Affleck

There's a lot of noise in the world, and the Internet magnifies that energy.

Ben Affleck

There's something really great and romantic about being poor and sleeping on couches.

Ben Affleck

To answer the question, though: I didn't always want to direct. I just liked the idea of it. If a friend was making a short and needed someone who knew screen direction, I would jump in. It would be horrible, but it led to a short, then another, and another. It was like student films.

Ben Affleck

Well I've never used that phrase before, but yes she is bootylicious.

Ben Affleck

What happens is this sort of bleed-over from the tabloids across your movie work. You go to a movie, you only go once. But the tabloids and Internet are everywhere. You can really subsume the public image of somebody.

Ben Affleck

When I look up at the screen and see myself I always have to laugh. Not because I think I'm doing a horrible job, quite the contrary, I just feel it's so surreal to feel like one person can entertain so many at one time.

Ben Affleck

When I watch a guy I know is a big Republican, part of me thinks I probably wouldn't like this person if I met him, or we would have different opinions.

Ben Affleck

Yes, I'm going to be the President of the United States. You know why? You think you can get chicks by being in the movies? You can really get chicks by being the President.

Ben Affleck

You can say what you want about me. You can yell at me with a video camera and be TMZ. You can follow me around and take pictures all you want. I don't care.

Ben Affleck

You get old, you slow down.

Ben Affleck

You have to look also to the media, where you have a vast majority of the loudest and most influential political voices in America media from people who came from the entertainment world.

Ben Affleck

You know George M. Steinbrenner III is the center of all evil in the universe.

Ben Affleck

You're basically the sum of all the experiences you've ever had, and they're sort of shaken up in you and reproduced in the things you create, and that includes seeing movies.

Ben Affleck

This page is intentionally left blank

This page is intentionally left blank

This page is intentionally left blank

This page is intentionally left blank

This page is intentionally left blank

www.ingramcontent.com/pod-product-compliance
Lightning Source LLC
Chambersburg PA
CBHW061949280526
45787CB00004B/1779